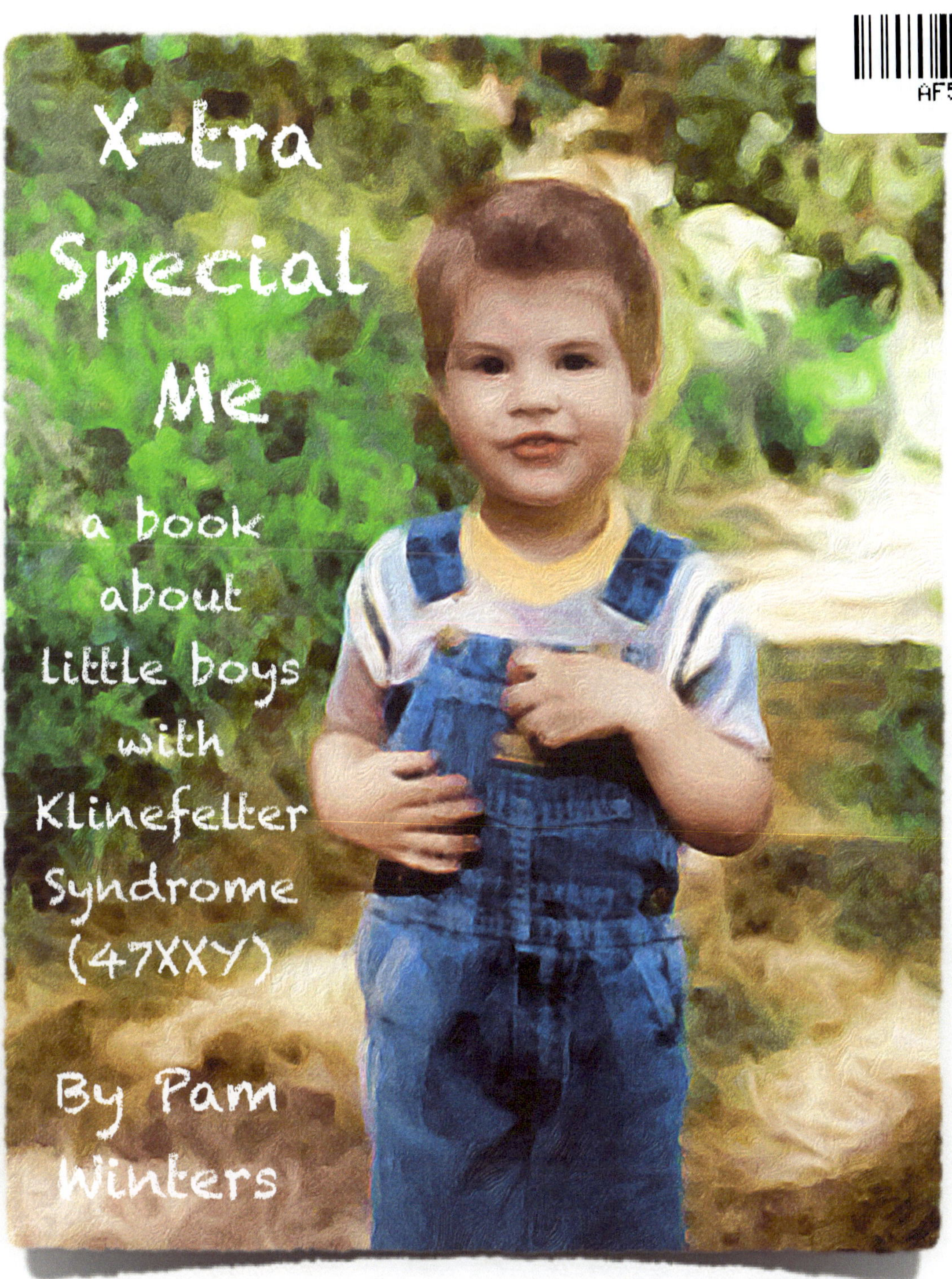
X-tra
Special
Me

a book
about
Little boys
with
Klinefelter
Syndrome
(47XXY)

By Pam
Winters

AF507163

X-tra Special Me

a book about little boys
with Klinefelter Syndrome
(47XXY)

by Pam Winters

To my son, Brian, who was diagnosed with Klinefelter Syndrome at the age of 31. May all the little boys diagnosed with 47XXY in utero know from the start that they are "x-tra special".

When I was born,
or so I'm told,
my parents looked
at me and said,

"He's perfect."

An easy baby I would be,
slept through the night
by just week three.

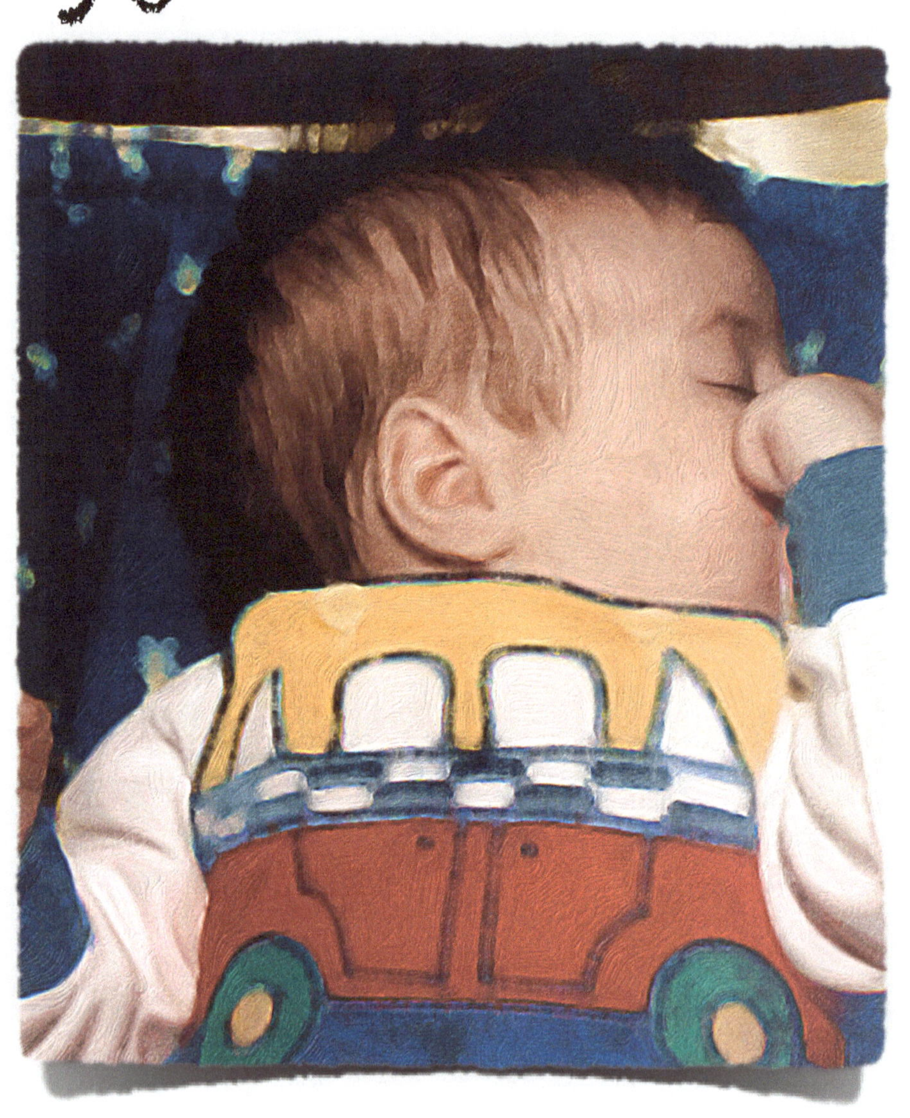

It made my parents think that I was someone

x-tra special.

I learned to crawl and walk and play. I took my time, but that's ok.

Content and happy I would sit, observed the world, just couldn't quit.

It made my parents think that I was someone x-tra special.

I like to try to do new things, I'll take a chance to spread my wings.

So please be patient, please be kind. I might need time to just unwind.

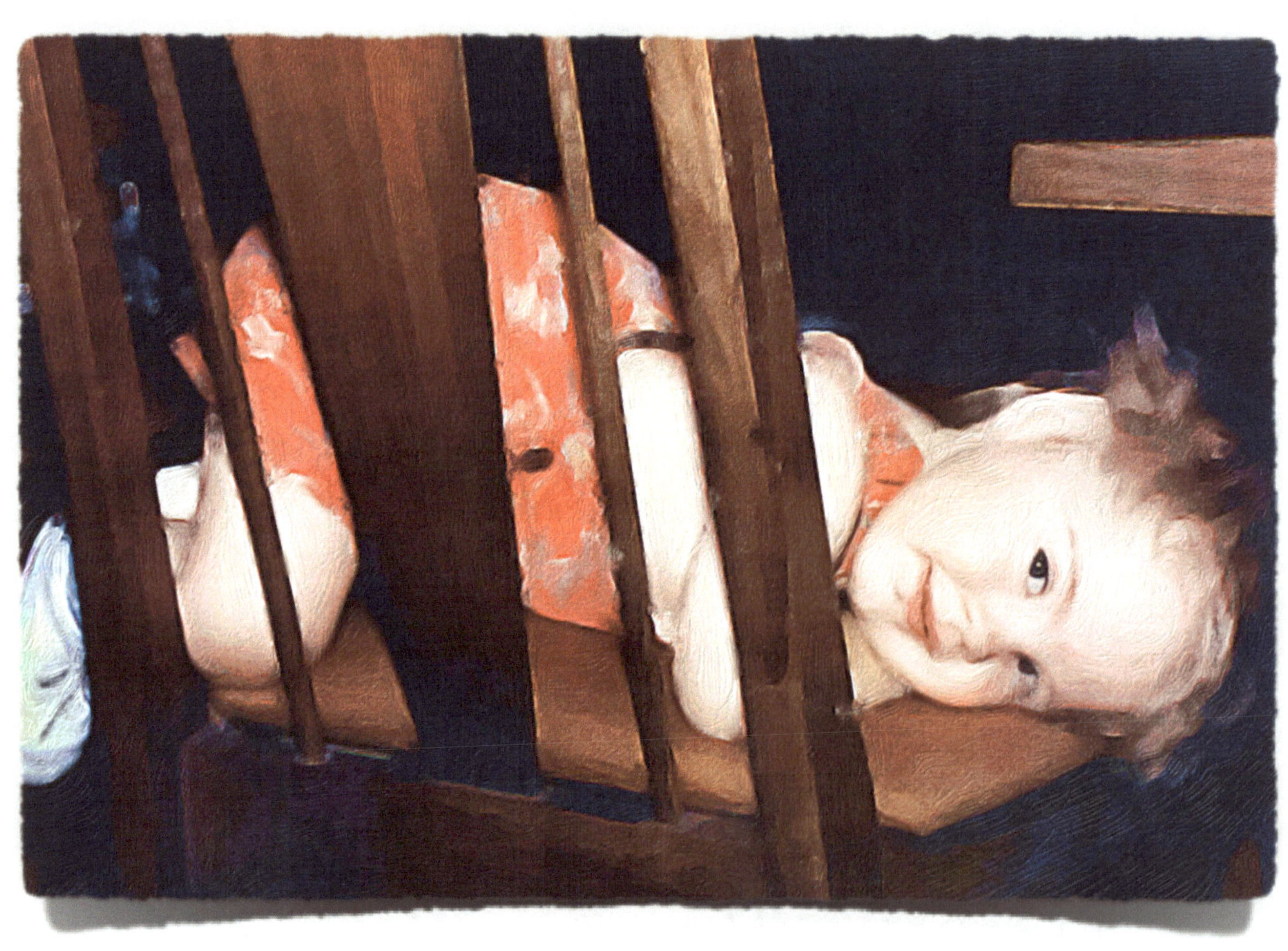

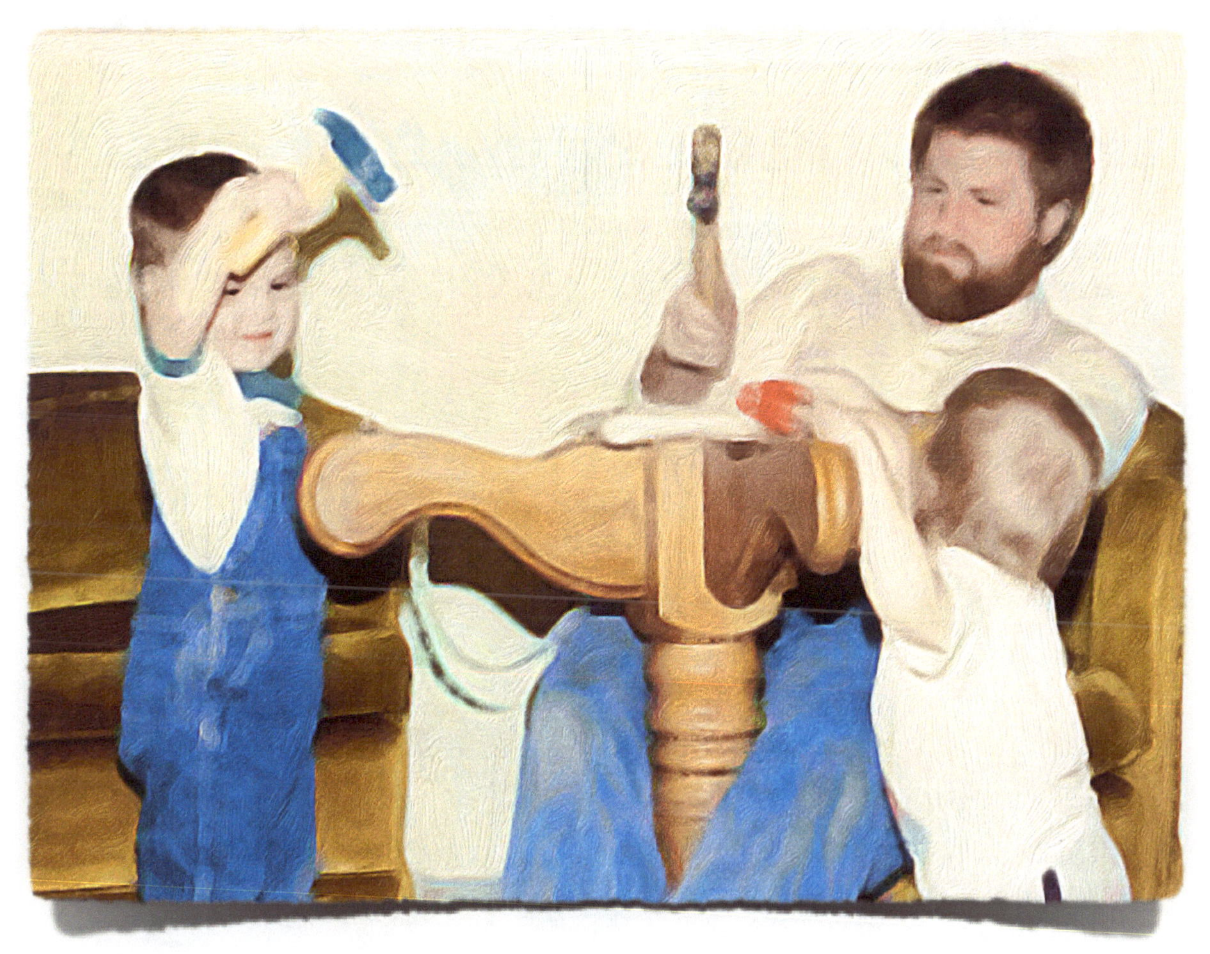

I draw and build. I sing and dance. I do my best when given a chance.

I smile. I laugh. I hug
and squeeze. But mostly
I just want to please.

It makes my parents think that I am someone x-tra special.

Strong feelings do inside me live. Sometimes they make me sensitive.

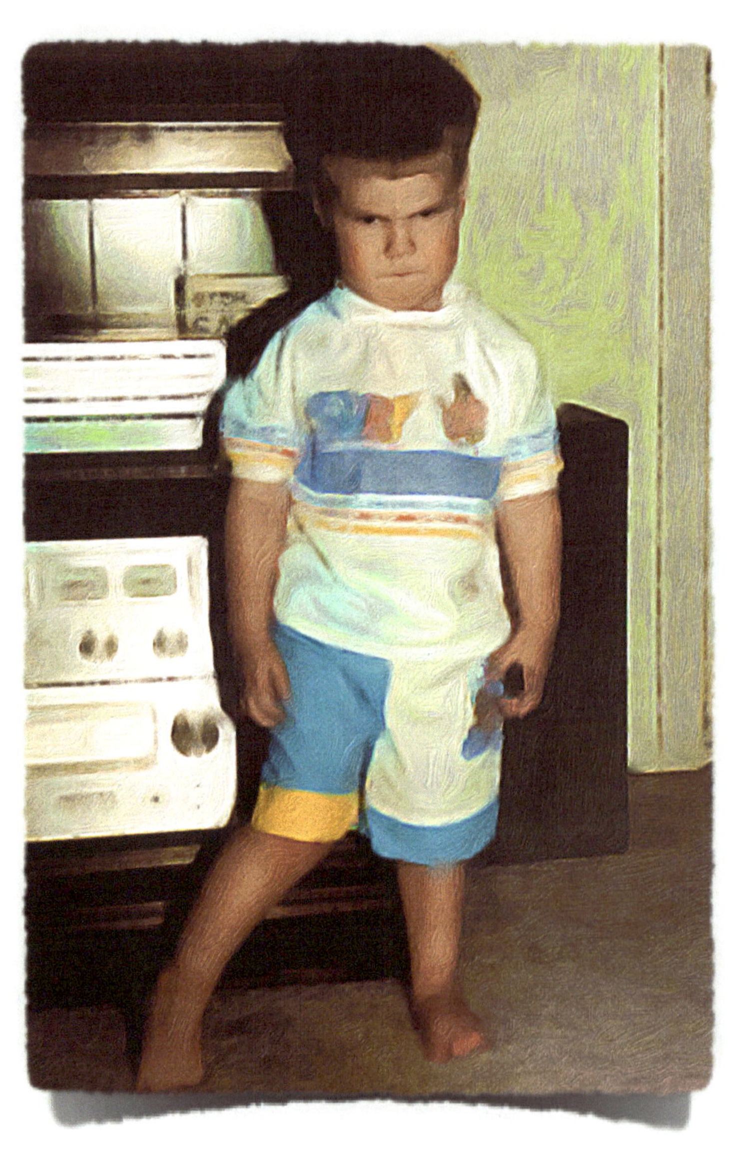

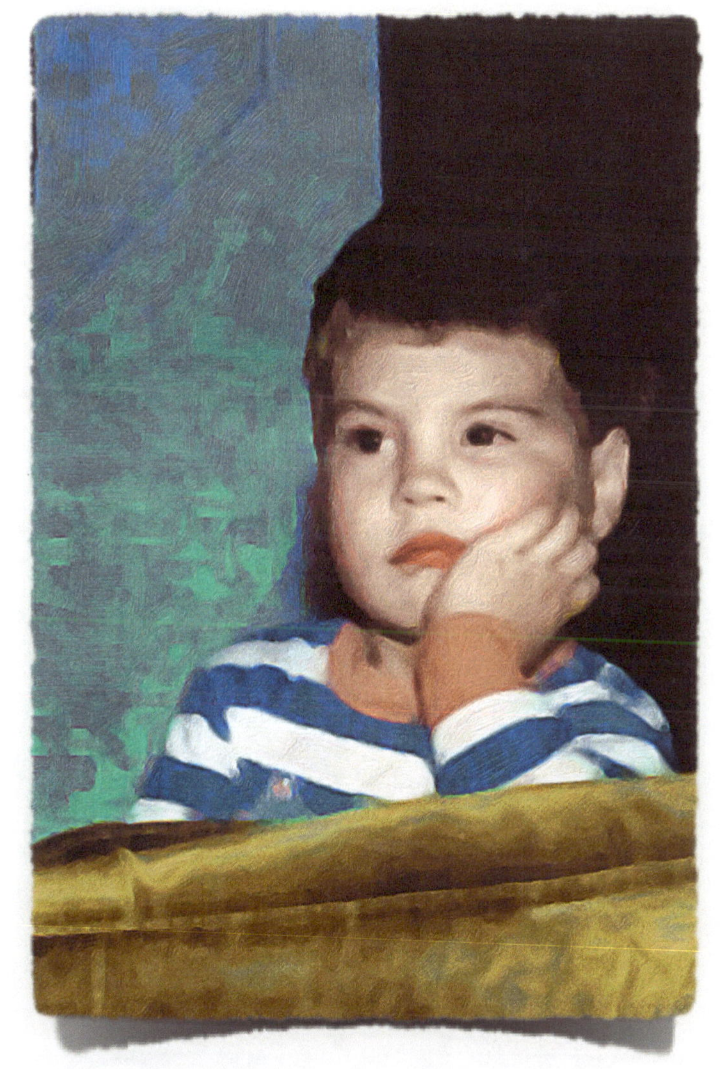

Emotions help me
empathize. Sometimes
that's hard for kids my size.

It makes my parents think that I am someone x-tra special.

I want to see who I can be.
I want to be uniquely me.

So here is something you
should know. I'll tell you
now before you go.

Have you ever
heard of
chromosomes?
In 23 pairs they
make their homes.

Inside us, there
are 46, in every
body cell.

But WAIT!
There's something
more to tell.

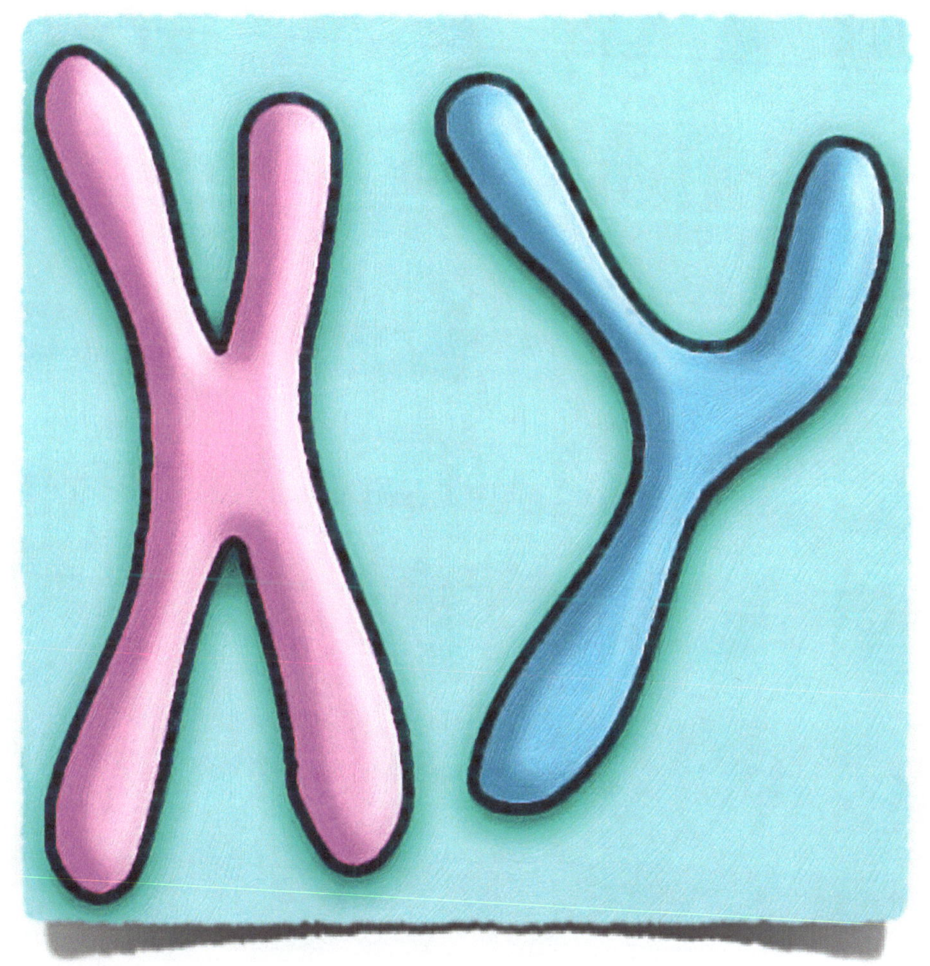

Keep listening, you have
to try. Most boys they
have an X and Y.

There are some boys, though, just like me. They have an extra X, you see.

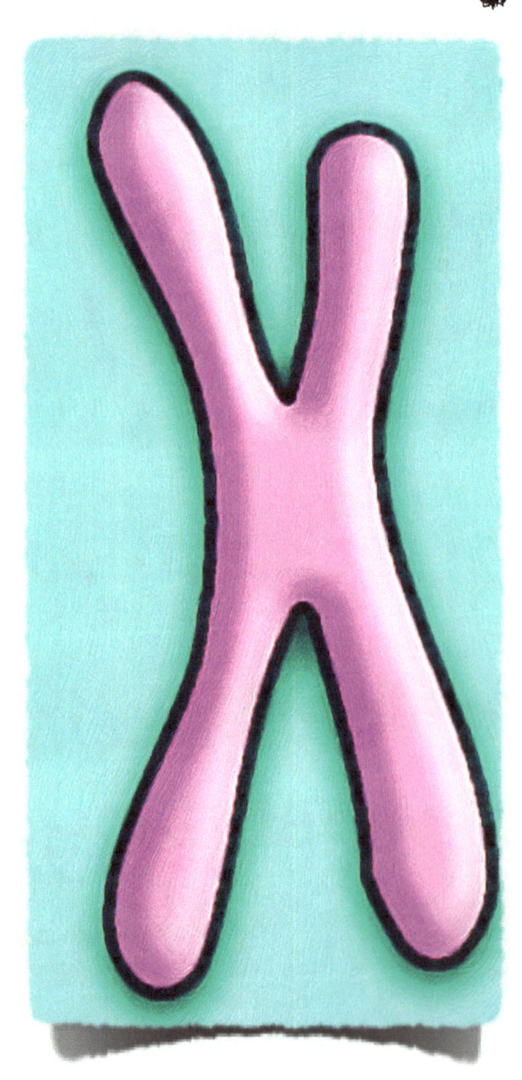

It has a name.
It's really long,
discovered by
this guy.

If Klinefelter
is hard to say,
just call it...

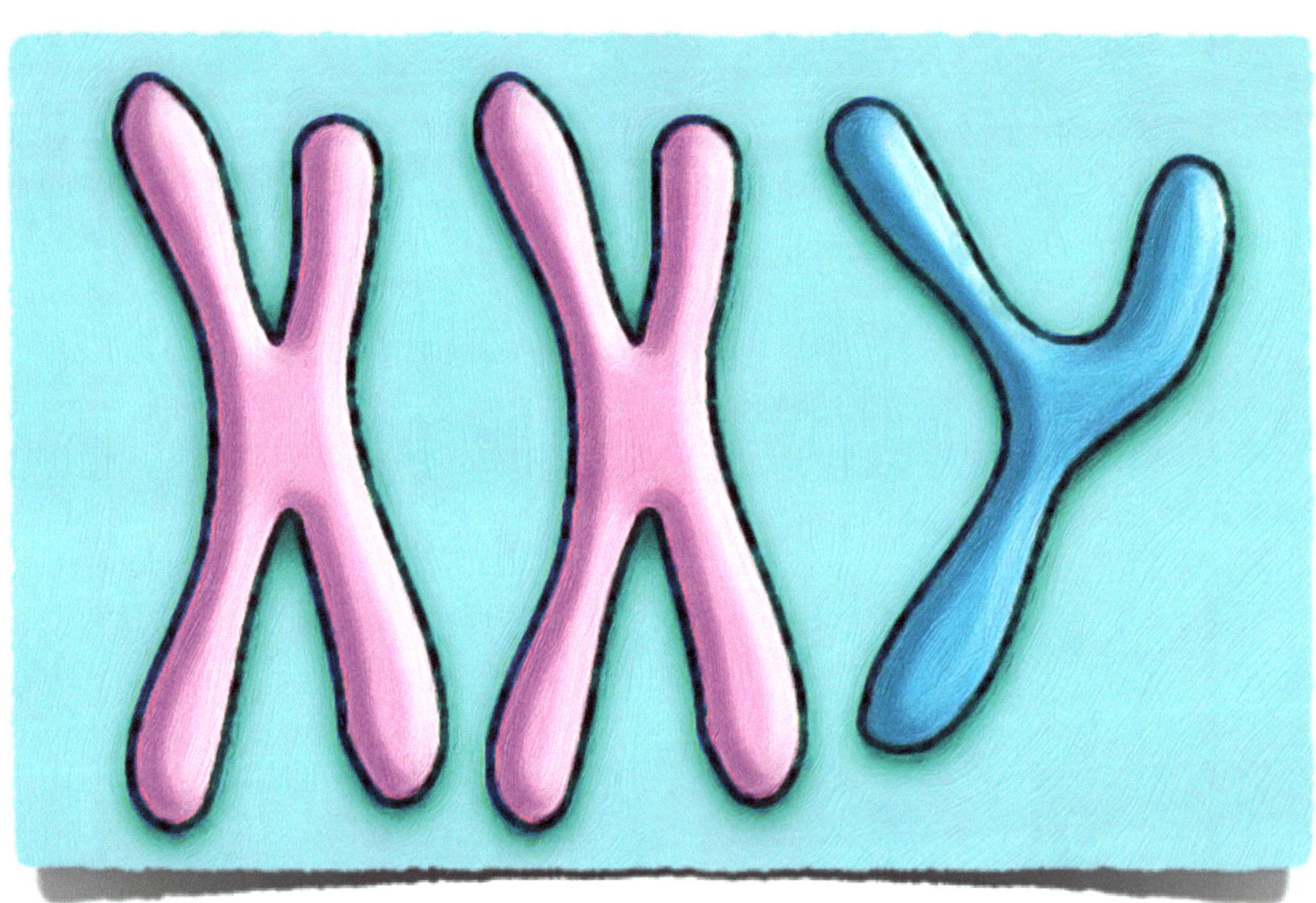

So, now you know what
makes me, me.

But is there
something more?

I guess you'll have to
wait and see,
what more I have
in store.

Because it's true,
I cant deny, with this
I cannot wrestle,

That all along my parents
KNEW that I am someone
x-tra special!

From the Author

Even before entering the world, Brian let Joe and me know whose timeline we'd be following once he arrived. After four grueling days of being induced, our perfect baby boy was born. He was an easy baby and toddler. Brian slept well, was highly verbal, and was always very happy. Eventually, he did struggle in school, both academically and socially. Throughout his life, though, Brian has fought to overcome his challenges. He's worked hard to become a healthier person, both physically and emotionally.

Recently, I connected with the non-profit organization, Living with XXY. Their mission is to raise awareness about Klinefelter Syndrome by sharing the success stories of males around the world who were born with an extra X chromosome. By doing so, their hope is to dispel all of the negative, outdated information that continues to be spread, not only by what's out there on the internet, but also by the medical community. Scientific advances in recent years have now made it easier to diagnose Klinefelter Syndrome in utero. By writing this book, I hope to give parents of little boys with 47XXY a tool that will help them celebrate everything that makes their sons "x-tra special".

 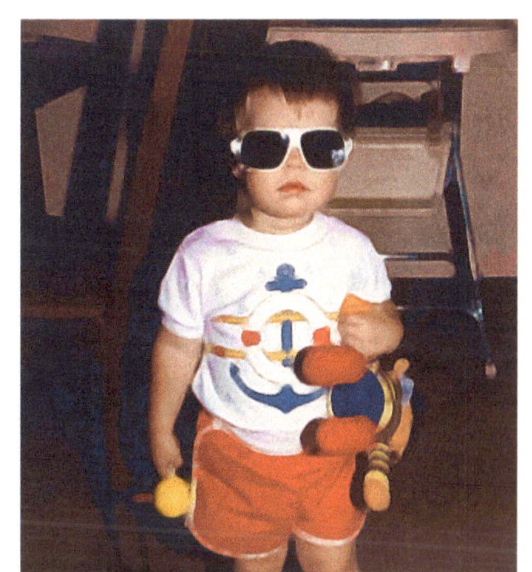 

All net proceeds from this project will be donated to Living with XXY.